The Stations of the Cross

Detail of Crucifix at the Church of St. Croix
Kaysersberg, Alsace, France

The Stations of the Cross

Photographs and Meditations

Paul E. Hoffman

WIPF & STOCK · Eugene, Oregon

THE STATIONS OF THE CROSS
Photographs and Meditations

Wipf and Stock
An Imprint of Wipf and Stock Publishers
199 W. 8th Ave., Suite 3
Eugene, OR 97401
www.wipfandstock.com

ISBN 13: 978-1-61097-119-5

Manufactured in the U.S.A.

For Mom and Dad
The first ones to show me the way of the cross

Contents

Introduction

SINCE ANCIENT times, faithful followers of Jesus have found following in his Good Friday steps a meaningful and spiritually enriching devotional practice. To be able to do so in Jerusalem was an honor of such magnitude that the perils of travel from far northern European locations were not thought too high a price to pay. But since not everyone could afford the time nor the expense of such a trip, local parishes began setting up the pathway to the cross within their own worship spaces. Then the faithful could recall and give thanks for the journey that Christ made on behalf of all humanity to the cross on that final Friday of his earthly life. Evidence of such "stations" can be traced to the Franciscans, who most likely set up their original stations outdoors for local Lenten devotions.

Station 8, Jesus dies on the Cross from The Church of Notre
Dame and St. Stephen Romorantin-Lathenay, France

During a recent trip to Western Europe, I was fascinated by the centrality that the stations played in the architecture and overall design of its cathedrals and churches, both large and small. The style and ornamentation of the stations was sometimes so intrinsic to the building's overall design that they seemed effortless in their communication of the way of the cross. In other cases, they made bold and vivid statements about the place of this piety in Christian life by their stark contrast to their surroundings. In one case, they were the last vestige of an otherwise abandoned parish church. While the pews were ransacked and covered with dust and cobwebs, the stations, simple though they were, hung out of reach of vandals and others who had done as they wished with the abandoned house of prayer.

The visits to these churches—primarily in France and England—had a profound impact on me as I contemplated the millions of Christians who, over the years and across the globe, had retraced Jesus' steps en route to his death and final, victorious resurrection. Having celebrated the Stations of the Cross for over twenty-five years at noon on Good Friday, the photos and meditations I offer here are an expansion of that annual liturgy. They are meant to be used throughout the Lenten season or whenever it seems appropriate to the reader to pause to contemplate the gift of Christ to a fallen world. They are meant as well to offer a glimpse into the diversity and beauty of a small segment of Western Christendom's interpretations and representations of Jesus' final walk.

The number of the stations has been in transition since their origin. Presently the most typical number in Roman Catholic practice is fourteen stations, so mandated by Pope Clement XII in 1731. While the number fourteen continues to be most common in catholic practice, *which* fourteen is significantly shifting. As recently as 2007, Pope Benedict XVI proposed a more Biblically centered set of stations for Roman practice. However, with the 1731 traditional stations' artwork so prominent in churches across the world it may be quite some time until these newer proposals become common practice.

Protestant congregations tend toward ten stations, all of which have Biblical references in the Gospels with the exception of Station Three, Jesus Falls, which relies on Psalm 118 to bring scriptural legitimacy to it. As a Lutheran pastor, my tradition and practice has been with the use of the ten stations, which is therefore the content of this set of photos and meditations.

And I, when I am lifted up from earth
will draw all people to myself. (John 12:32)
Damaged Crucifix
Paroisse Notre Dame
Villedieu-les-Poêles
Normandy, France

Station One

Jesus is condemned to death before Pilate

Now Jesus stood before the governor; and the governor asked him, 'Are you the King of the Jews?' Jesus said, 'You say so.' But when he was accused by the chief priests and elders, he did not answer. Then Pilate said to him, 'Do you not hear how many accusations they make against you?' But he gave him no answer, not even to a single charge, so that the governor was greatly amazed.

Now at the festival the governor was accustomed to release a prisoner for the crowd, anyone whom they wanted. At that time they had a notorious prisoner, called Jesus Barabbas. So after they had gathered, Pilate said to them, 'Whom do you want me to release for you, Jesus Barabbas or Jesus who is called the Messiah?' For he realized that it was out of jealousy that they had handed him over. While he was sitting on the judgment seat, his wife sent word to him, 'Have nothing to do with that innocent man, for today I have suffered a great deal because of a dream about him.' Now the chief priests and the elders persuaded the crowds to ask for Barabbas and to have Jesus killed. The governor again said to them, 'Which of the two do you want me to release for you?' And they said, 'Barabbas.' Pilate said to them, 'Then what should I do with Jesus who is called the Messiah?' All of them said, 'Let him be crucified!' Then he asked, 'Why, what evil has he done?' But they shouted all the more, 'Let him be crucified!'

So when Pilate saw that he could do nothing, but rather that a riot was beginning, he took some water and washed his hands before the crowd, saying, 'I am innocent of this man's blood; see to it yourselves.' Then the people as a whole answered, 'His blood be on us and on our children!' So he released Barabbas for them; and after flogging Jesus, he handed him over to be crucified.

—MATTHEW 27:11–26

IN THIS contemporary, family-oriented parish of Sacré-Coeur (Sacred Heart) in the Parisian suburb of Ris-Orangis, the stations are hand-crafted by members of the congregation. Their representation of the fourteen stations were produced over the period of a Lenten season as a devotional practice and were each fabricated by a small group of multi-generational parishioners working together. One must assume that there was some sort of over-all collaboration and design coordination since each station portrays Christ in similar off-white broken tiles of eight to ten pieces.

~

If, however, you bite and devour one another, take care that
you are not consumed by one another.

—GALATIANS 5:15

It is a common experience in most every elementary school classroom and on every elementary school playground that when there is trouble, the accuser and the accused often become interchanged. In the heat of the moment of being caught, confusion abounds and the "he said, she said" is difficult for even the most experienced classroom teacher to sort out.

As we grow older, we move on from the elementary school classroom, but the difficulty in sorting out who is at fault between the accuser and the accused continues to be baffling, often completely elusive.

As Jesus stands before Pilate, it is clear that Jesus is the accused, but not so clear who are the accusers. And for Pilate, there is no clarity about exactly what the accusations are, either. The cast of characters expands, as it often does in the classroom or boardroom when things are out of control, and with the growing cast comes growing uncertainty. Pilate's wife, the notorious prisoner, Barabbas, and the gathering crowd all contribute to a mob mentality where chaos reigns.

One of the prayers for this station of the liturgy proclaims, "And Christ, who on the last day will judge the living and the dead, is himself judged before Pilate."

There could be no clearer explanation of who is judging whom. Today the innocent Jesus is judged at the hand of a guilty humanity. But the journey of the cross that Christ is about to take will bring clarity for all time. The victory of the cross and resurrection will seal the world's future with the imprint of the Gospel and we will confess across the centuries, "He will come again to judge the living and the dead." He will judge. Jesus. It is clear.

When we find ourselves in moments of judgment both big and small, it is helpful to remember that no matter how thick the haze of confusion that hangs over our situation, it is Christ who is the loving, compassionate ruler of all things. By standing in our place before the powers of the world, he who was judged becomes the one, in the end, who judges all. His judgments are steeped in the mercy of justice. His fairness exceeds all that we know as humanly fair.

The opportunity to extend to others the mercy shown to us by Christ who will come again to judge the living and the dead is a gift that the cross of Jesus offers to the faithful.

From the classroom to the boardroom, from the courtroom to the bedroom, the people of God can raise their voices in confident thanksgiving and praise to the one whose judgments are steeped in mercy.

⁓

Gracious God, to you alone belongs the wisdom to see through the chaos and turmoil of human lives to that which is true and just. We give you thanks for your compassionate judgment of the world, and your acceptance of our need to be reconciled to you and to one another. Help us in our weakness to reach to others with the compassion and mercy that you share with us so freely.

We ask this through Christ our Lord. Amen.

Station Two

Jesus receives the cross

Now it was the day of Preparation for the Passover; and it was about noon. He said to the Jews, 'Here is your King!' They cried out, 'Away with him! Away with him! Crucify him!' Pilate asked them, 'Shall I crucify your King?' The chief priests answered, 'We have no king but the emperor.' Then he handed him over to them to be crucified.

So they took Jesus; and carrying the cross by himself, he went out to what is called The Place of the Skull, which in Hebrew is called Golgotha.

—John 19:14–17

IN THE Church of Sainte-Marie-Madeleine, just off the central square plaza in Belgium, one finds these simple yet profound renderings of the Stations of the Cross. Fabricated from materials that make them look almost like animated figures, they clearly describe the actions of Jesus and the other characters of the passion narratives.

The Grand'Place, Brussels

~

Bear one another's burdens
and in this way you fulfill the law of Christ.

—GALATIANS 6:2

The day that my mother-in-law died, only her three children and I were still at the hospital with her. So it fell to us to return to the family home and share the news with her husband of fifty-four years. Even her will and determination was no match for the stroke she had suffered several days before. She was gone.

On the way home, the four of us stopped at a convenience store to pick up a few sandwiches since none of us had eaten much in the last 24 hours, and we knew that dad hadn't either. Several times throughout the coming week, we returned to that Plaid Pantry in our conversations. We talked about how odd it seemed to each of us that even though we were experiencing a life-changing event, others in the store were simply going about their daily routines, buying chips and pop, picking up lottery tickets, paying for gas, earning a living. No one knew the burden we were carrying.

It was not unusual for a convict to pass through the streets of Jerusalem carrying a cross on the way to his execution. As such a procession passed, women continued the daily routine of walking to the well, men crafted wood or leather into tools and sold or traded them. Children played in the streets.

Even though this particular Friday it was Jesus, few were aware of the significance of the cross that he bore. And no one could possibly have known of the burdens that he carried on his shoulders—the sins of the world: past, present, and future. Christ carried nothing of his own and all that was and is ours on that lonely way from Pilate's chambers to Golgotha's executioners. Fully human, he offered himself for us, a gift for which we can be forever grateful.

The opportunity to offer our gratitude in all circumstances is a gift that the cross of Jesus offers to the faithful.

One of the ways that our gratitude might take shape is through a heightened awareness of those around us for whom Christ died and the burdens that they are carrying every day. Silently, quietly, and without our awareness, there is a world full of people in the convenience store, the next cubicle, beside us in the classroom or the boardroom, on the street or at the stadium. Wherever there are people, there are people who are hurting, people for whom Christ carried the cross.

For those both near and far whose burdens are known or unknown, to extend ourselves in love is to extend the arms of Christ.

Christ carried the cross on behalf of all the world's people. Our thoughtful care shared with others is a faithful response of gratitude for what Christ has done for us. It also reflects our God-given awareness that the cross was not only carried for me, or for some, but for all. He carried it even, perhaps especially, for those who appear to just be picking up a few things at Plaid Pantry on an ordinary day.

∾

Gracious God, you bore the sins of the world on the bruised shoulders of Jesus. We give thanks to you for love so great and merciful, extended to all the world. Help us to reach to others with your love, extending ourselves to those whose suffering and pain is sometimes visible, but often hidden.

We ask this through Christ our Lord. Amen.

STATION THREE

Jesus falls

I was pushed hard, so that I was falling,
But the LORD helped me.
The LORD is my strength and my might;
he has become my salvation.

—PSALM 118:13–14

THESE STUNNING gold-bordered stations are found in the Cathedral of Sées in Normandy, France. Hung on walls that show the wear of age in this war-battered cathedral, the beauty of these mosaics stands in stark contradictions to the horror of the events of Good Friday that they depict.

~

For as all die in Adam, so all will be made alive in Christ.

—FIRST CORINTHIANS 15:22

My grandfather began falling. All the time. Sometimes more than once in a day. When I was a boy, I had an elderly grandfather whose advancing years took their toll in weakened legs. Having been a stout and able farmer all his life, this was a hard fate for him to accept. It was so hard that his way of coping with his loss was denial. "I didn't fall." You could have just picked him up from the middle of the farm lane where he was struggling to get back on his feet and he would swear to you that he hadn't fallen. "Not at all. Nope. Didn't fall."

For most adults in most circumstances, falling is a humiliating experience. Whether on the ski slope or the sidewalk, a fall is perceived as a failure.

Jesus falls. There he is. Crushed beneath the weight of his agony and the cross. I suspect that even though this is not attested to in the Gospels, the tradition of Christ's collapse on the way to Calvary was our Christian forebears' way of suggesting that the weight of our broken lives was just too much to bear, even for the Son of God. Jesus fell. There was nothing left to do but to get up and take that weight of ours to the cross. Humiliating though it might have been, the only option was to put the world's sinful, suffering load to death and let God raise up a renewed creation in its place.

So Jesus falls. And it was not the end of the world. In fact, it was one of the first steps of the world's new beginning. The new Adam mimics the old Adam. Where once humanity fell, now God falls. Where once there was creation that human beings spurned, God now promises a new creation where divine love re-imagines.

The opportunity to see ourselves and others as frail human beings in need of re-creation in Christ is a gift that the cross of Jesus offers to the faithful.

I suspect that part of the denial that grandpa and all people feel is that the little falls remind us of the bigger fall. It is the biggest fall of all, that of falling away from God and God's purpose for our lives. The way of the cross is a gracious reminder that ours is a God whose love is broad enough to pick us up and redirect our lives, no matter how big or small our sprawling missteps might be.

~

Gracious God, you were not ashamed to take on the nature of the human family, nor to suffer the fall in order to bring us back in grace into your loving arms. Be with us in this journey of life, boldly embracing its peaks and valleys in the confidence of your crucified hands leading and guiding us along the way.

We ask this through Christ our Lord. Amen.

Station Four

The cross is laid on Simon

They compelled a passer-by, who was coming in from the country, to carry his cross; it was Simon of Cyrene, the father of Alexander and Rufus.

—Mark 15:21

O FTEN LOST in the shadow of its cousin down the street, Westminster *Abbey,* the Roman Catholic Cathedral in Westminster, is built in the Byzantine style and is replete with mosaics depicting the events of Scripture and the life of Christ. Placed on the pillars that support this massive structure, the beautifully carved limestone reliefs of each station are adorned with gold leafing that forms a halo around Christ's head and a cross atop each station. The fourteen stations of the cathedral, each five feet eight inches square, are the work of renowned British artist Eric Gill.

~

*So if anyone is in Christ, there is a new creation: everything old
has passed away; see, everything has become new!*

—SECOND CORINTHIANS 5:17

In the summer of 1974, I spent twelve weeks abroad as a
foreign exchange student in Kabul, Afghanistan along with
sixteen other American high school students. After ten days
of intense orientation in both New York City and Istanbul,
the seventeen of us landed at the Kabul airport, were met
by our host families and quickly whisked into private cars,
taxis, or bicycles for our separate journeys to what was
about to become home.

The next hour was unbelievable. Our driver sped reck-
lessly through the city's streets, streets that were teeming
with pedestrians, camels, shepherds and their flocks, some
other cars, and bicyclists. In the air swirled honking horns,
bleating animals, blaring music. There were more times
than I could count that we came within inches of another
car, or a pedestrian, a biker, some sheep. It was a ride I will
never forget.

By the time we reached our family compound and
servants came to open the gate at the honking of our car
horn, I had seen fresh meat hanging in the open air market,
women roaming the streets completely covered in burqas,
brilliantly painted trucks, mosques, breathtaking surrounding mountains.

This is not what I was expecting. It was clear I wasn't
in southern Pennsylvania anymore, and that I was eighteen
and incredibly alone. I had no idea when I would see one

of my new American friends again. Though I didn't know it at the time, I was in shock—culture shock. And I stayed in one level or another of this state of shock for several days, maybe even weeks. To cross from one culture to another in such a short period of time was too much for me. This sort of disorientation happens whenever one is taken from their own native way of thinking and experiencing life and is transported into something entirely new.

It must be the sort of thing that happened to Simon of Cyrene when one day in Jerusalem he found his world completed transformed when he went from passer-by to cross-bearer. This is not what he was expecting. Certainly his first reaction would have been to assume that he himself was about to be crucified. The raging mob and efficient executioners were not the sort of crowd to get mixed up in. But in truth, when Simon was given the cross, he was about to be crucified, but not in the way he expected. Instead he received through the cross the opportunity to put all that was sin and death behind him. Life was about to be transformed, not taken away. He was in a cross cultural moment, a moment Christ offers to all. The way of Christ transports us from a culture of death to a culture of life. First Christ shoulders the sins of the world on his own; then the cross becomes for every Simon in human history a place where the old is carried away to Calvary. In Easter's empty tomb, behold! the new has come.

The opportunity to have Christ put to death all that is death in us is a gift that the cross of Jesus offers to the faithful.

It is a cross cultural experience. It takes a bit to get used to it. It is shocking, transforming, and true.

❧

Gracious God, we give thanks to you that through your servant Simon you give us the courage to cast the burden of our sinful lives onto the same cross that he carried. Make us worthy to walk by your side in bearing the burdens of others, and upright in receiving the new life that is offered in no place other than your cross.

We ask this through Christ our Lord. Amen.

STATION FIVE

The women of Jerusalem weep

A great number of the people followed him, and among them were women who were beating their breasts and wailing for him. But Jesus turned to them and said, "Daughters of Jerusalem, do not weep for me, but weep for yourselves and for your children. For the days are surely coming when they will say, 'Blessed are the barren, and the wombs that never bore, and the breasts that never nursed.'

—LUKE 23:27–29

In the very traditional church of Our Lady of the Assumption in the village of Cormatin in Burgundy, one finds these stunning representations of the fourteen stations.

The artist is Jean-Paul Longin, a native of this region of Burgundy. He prepared the installation in the early 1990's. The medium is charcoal and pastel on paper, matted and framed. The artist is obviously influenced by the mystery and mysticism of the cross of Christ. He enjoys working with form, light, and structure, all of which he refers to as gifts of the Spirit.

So teach us to count our days that we may gain a wise heart.

—Psalm 90:12

A few Christmases ago at the congregation I serve, there was an unsettling discovery. About the second Sunday of Advent or so, the Christmas costumes appeared to be AWOL. Missing. Vanished without a trace. Bathrobes-turned-shepherd-suits and diaphanous angel wings absolutely unaccounted for.

I had a hunch about this, but for once in my life I kept my mouth shut and just watched it all unravel from the sidelines.

It wasn't until the last Sunday in April that the mystery was solved and the hens came home to roost on this one. The last Sunday of April is the Sunday that all the Lutheran World Relief quilts are draped across the pews on Sunday morning for their blessing before being loaded and shipped to parts unknown.

And there in the patchwork they were. A little bit of the Virgin Mary's blue in this quilt, a bit of Shepherd robe in that quilt. Upholstery fabric once fit for a king now cut and pieced into a gift for a pauper.

It was an honest mistake. The quilters' storage and the costume storage share the same space. The ladies in their Tuesday morning commitment to make all things new simply assumed that these were just one more set of donated fabric goods, the scissors did their terrible deed, and the rest, as they say, is history.

Can you imagine a better use for the swaddling clothes of Christ than to actually swaddle a child of God in need beneath the quilted cover of such love and grace? When the shock and sadness of what was lost wore off, even those who had devoted hours to the careful crafting of costumes for the crèche could see the fortuitous outcome of the unintentional re-appropriation of their original handiwork.

"Behold! I will make all things new," the one seated on the throne declares. "Write this, for these words are trustworthy and true."

To the women of Jerusalem, on this day of days, Jesus says, "be careful that your priorities are aligned in the spirit of the Gospel."

The opportunity to order life's priorities to serve those in need is a gift that the cross of Jesus offers to the faithful.

Even the most mundane tasks in life are deserving of our careful thought as we seek to pattern our lives in the way of the cross. "How can I offer what Christ has so freely given, in order to bring justice and joy into the world?"

~

*Gracious God, your words and acts of love encourage us to give
ourselves freely for the needs of others, just as you have done.
By your grace and presence with us as our risen Lord, assist
us in the choices we make. So order our days and our deeds in
your peace that we may be wise and generous in all that we say
and do, in every choice we make.*

We ask this through Christ our Lord. Amen.

Station Six

Jesus is stripped of his garments

When the soldiers had crucified Jesus, they took his clothes and divided them into four parts, one for each soldier. They also took his tunic; now the tunic was seamless, woven in one piece from the top. So they said to one another, 'Let us not tear it, but cast lots for it to see who will get it.' This was to fulfill what the scripture says, 'They divided my clothes among themselves, and for my clothing they cast lots.' And that is what the soldiers did. Meanwhile, standing near the cross of Jesus were his mother, and his mother's sister, Mary the wife of Clopas, and Mary Magdalene.

—John 19:23–25

THE PARISH of Notre-Dame de Ris-Orangis is located in a bustling, modern suburb south of Paris. The present church was built in 1868 in response to the doubling population of this town in the mid-nineteenth century. Its architecture is neo-Roman, typical of the time period, and its detailed stations in gray scale on navy background are also period pieces.

⌒

*So you also must consider yourselves dead to sin
and alive to God in Christ Jesus.*

—ROMANS 6:11

When Arno was baptized, his parents chose to have him fully immersed, totally naked. This is not the usual state of affairs in Lutheran churches for infant baptisms although many post-modern churches are returning to this ancient practice to re-capture in fuller measure the drama of dying to sin and rising to new life. For some reason on that Sunday I was wearing a large pectoral cross, something that I do not often do, but the entire congregation and I were about to find out why.

As Arno emerged from the waters of baptism following the words, "I baptize you in the name of the Father, and of the Son, and of the Holy Spirit," his tiny hand took hold of that cross. And he would not let go. As he was signed with the cross of Jesus, as he was sealed in the Holy Spirit with the oil, he continued to hang on tight. I was about to re-learn a lesson since forgotten from the time when my own children were infants: an infant's grasp can be amazingly firm and determined.

To exacerbate the humiliation of execution by crucifixion, the soldiers stripped Christ of his garments. In the end there was nothing left to cling to but the cross itself. Everything was taken away, and it was not until he was already elevated above the gazes of the rude multitude that the soldiers held in their own hands the evidence of the purity and wholeness of this stranger they had stripped. "... now the tunic was seamless, woven in one piece from the top." Soon through his own death and resurrection the naked Christ would restore the innocence of the naked Adam and Eve in the Garden of Eden, naked, whole, and unashamed.

We all still tell Arno the story of his baptism.

"Just as one finger was pried away another took hold."

"It was amazing how you hung on to the cross when you came up out of those waters."

"I thought I was going to have to hand both you and my cross back to your parents."

The opportunity to cling to the cross when we are stripped of everything else is a gift that the cross of Jesus offers to the faithful.

We all love to tell Arno his baptismal story not because it's cute or endearing, but because at its core it is the essence of what baptism is about. Stripped and helpless, Christ takes us out of this world as we were brought into it—with nothing. And as we emerge from the water's womb, we are reborn children of God and inheritors of eternal life. We are reborn children of the cross.

≈

Gracious God, we give thanks to you that in Jesus Christ you were clothed in the humanity of a fallen and broken world. As you were stripped of all things in heaven and on earth, you stripped us of all illusions, exposing our rebellion and sin. At the same time, you gave us a vision of the new creation wherein we are reborn to the beauty and splendor into which we were first intended by the Creator. Give us glad and generous hearts to cling always to your cross, the place of sin's death and the birth place of the New Creation.

We ask this through Christ our Lord. Amen.

STATION SEVEN

Jesus is nailed to the cross

It was nine o'clock in the morning when they crucified him. The inscription of the charge against him read, "The King of the Jews." And with him they crucified two bandits, one on his right and one on his left. Those who passed by derided him, shaking their heads and saying, "Aha! You who would destroy the temple and build it in three days, save yourself, and come down from the cross!" In the same way the chief priests, along with the scribes, were also mocking him among themselves and saying, "He saved others; he cannot save himself. Let the Messiah, the King of Israel, come down from the cross now, so that we may see and believe." Those who were crucified with him also taunted him.

—MARK 15:25–32

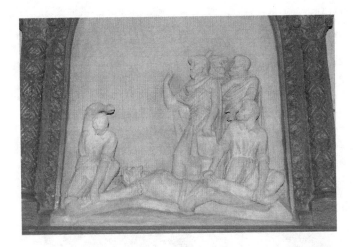

THE PARISH church in Romorantin-Lathenay in Central France is L'Eglise de Notre-Dame et St. Etienne—the church of Our Lady and St. Stephen. Its carved stations are each housed in a little cathedral of their own, setting them off against the surrounding pale walls into which they would otherwise blend. The church is filled with artwork of various periods and styles of which these stations are but one sampling. This church was founded in the 11th Century and has undergone many changes over the years since, many necessitated by war damage, particularly following The Hundred Years' War.

The brutality and violence of this station's story stand in stark contrast to the bucolic setting of the stations within the church, and the church's setting next to the Sauldre River in this peaceful town.

L'Eglise de Notre-Dame et St. Etienne

~

For now we see in a mirror, dimly,
but then we will see face to face.

—FIRST CORINTHIANS 13:12A

Early one February Saturday morning when I was fourteen, I woke to an unusual noise outside my bedroom window. When I raised the shade, I could hardly believe my eyes. Dozens of my parents' church and community friends were in our lane with loads of stones, wheelbarrow and shovels, re-building the washed out entrance to our farm. In the next room my dad lay dying of cancer. These men and women had come to assure that if he needed medical help an ambulance would be able to reach him. It was an amazing sight.

It was also a fast track to the truth that I could no longer avoid. Dad was dying. And there was a community right outside my bedroom window. They knew what I did not want to allow myself to know. There was no turning back.

Less than twenty-four hours prior to the nails being driven into his hands, Christ had sweated out the prayer in the Garden of Gethsemane, asking that there might be some other way. But with each blow the hammer emphasized the truth that even the Christ did not want to allow himself to know. There was no turning back. "Those who passed by derided him," the Scriptures tell us. Likely some of those who derided him at the foot of the cross had followed him, learned from him, sought healing from him, perhaps even welcomed him to Jerusalem a few days earlier. But now a new truth was being firmly inscribed into the story of God's endless love for the world. The truth was being inscribed with the nails of the cross. There is no turning back.

The opportunity to know the truth is a gift that the cross of Jesus offers to the faithful.

The truth I didn't want to know about my dad's terminal cancer was laid bare before me one Saturday morning. But in knowing that truth, I found other truth as well. We had been isolated and alone, stranded by an impassable road and helpless to do anything about it. But now the community of faith reconnected us, at a time of our greatest need. There was no turning back from that truth, either, and what a life-giving truth it was.

The cross does not reveal its truth all at once. Likely if it did, it would be too much to take in. But firmly attached by our God to the cross of Christ forever, the truth of unrelenting love and acceptance continues to dawn on us day after day.

∼

Gracious God, in the cross of Jesus you reveal the fullness of truth, the truth of your constant and unfailing love for all creation. So fix our lives where true joy is found that our lives may be a witness to that love. Help us day by day to be those who speak and act in the truth of your unchanging love.

We ask this through Christ our Lord. Amen.

STATION EIGHT

Jesus dies upon the cross

When it was noon, darkness came over the whole land until three in the afternoon. At three o'clock Jesus cried out with a loud voice, "Eloi, Eloi, lema sabachthani?" which means, "My God, my God, why have you forsaken me?" When some of the bystanders heard it, they said, "Listen, he is calling for Elijah." And someone ran, filled a sponge with sour wine, put it on a stick, and gave it to him to drink, saying, "Wait, let us see whether Elijah will come to take him down." Then Jesus gave a loud cry and breathed his last. And the curtain of the temple was torn in two, from top to bottom. Now when the centurion, who stood facing him, saw that in this way he breathed his last, he said, "Truly this man was God's Son!"

—MARK 15:33–39

THESE STATIONS hang simply and unobtrusively against the white brick wall of the town church in the modest village of Longny-au-Perche in Préaux du Perche, a region south of Normandy, France. The church, St. Anne's Parish, is located on the town square at 1 Rue Eglise (1 Church Street), an obviously active Catholic parish.

~

I consider the sufferings of this present time
not worth comparing with the glory about to be revealed to us.

—ROMANS 8:18

Years ago when the kids were small and everyone was younger, my mom was flying in for a visit on Good Friday afternoon. The plan was for me to pick her up at the airport and then we'd all worship together on Friday evening. But a thick layer of fog in Dallas stranded her mid-way in the Atlanta airport and now it looked as if it would be well after midnight before she arrived.

She wasn't all that upset about being delayed, but she really hated to miss Good Friday service. "Don't worry," I told her on the crackling payphone line from the Atlanta airport. "I know how the story ends. I can tell it to you on the way home from the airport."

But I lied. To my own mother.

We might think we know how the story ends but the fullness of the story of the death of Jesus is still revealing itself to us day after day, week after week, year after year from here to the end of time. The meaning of Jesus' death in our moments of triumph and tragedy, both individually and as a part of the larger community of faith, continues to open mysteriously before us. After all, how can one say with any certainty what the death of Christ means? At best we can stand in awe and wonder and give thanks.

Just as soon as we think we have grasped the whole of it, God reveals yet another dimension of the depth and breadth and height of eternal love for us. Nowhere is this seen more fully and richly than in the cross.

The opportunity to enter into the mystery of love that knows no limits is a gift that the cross of Jesus offers to the faithful.

Not only on Good Friday, but every day of our lives God offers us the open arms of the Christ, extended in love, all the way to his dying breath. What is left for us but to stand in awe and wonder, and give thanks?

Together, we proclaim the mystery of faith:

Christ has died.

Christ is risen.

Christ will come again.

~

Gracious God, we give you thanks for the mystery and wonder of the cross, and for your saving death for each of us and for all of creation. As you continue to reveal yourself to us day by day, assist us as we grow in our love for you and for one another. Give us hearts that are thankful for the gift beyond measure, the gift of your very self.

We ask this through Christ our Lord. Amen

Station Nine

Jesus is taken down from the cross

And when all the crowds who had gathered there for this spectacle saw what had taken place, they returned home, beating their breasts. But all his acquaintances, including the women who had followed him from Galilee, stood at a distance, watching these things.

Now there was a good and righteous man named Joseph, who, though a member of the council, had not agreed to their plan and action. He came from the Jewish town of Arimathea, and he was waiting expectantly for the kingdom of God. This man went to Pilate and asked for the body of Jesus. Then he took it down, wrapped it in a linen cloth, and laid it in a rock-hewn tomb where no one had ever been laid.

—Luke 23:48–53

THIS IS not a station per se but an isolated artwork on a side wall in the town church in Kaysersberg, Alsace, France. It is easy to lose track of such small, individual works in this church dominated by the intricately carved high altar which is typical of this part of France and highly influenced by the neighboring Germans. A detailed portion of the overall high altar design is pictured below. Over the years this village and many like it in the Alsatian region have been in the hands of both French and German leadership. The region therefore reflects the rich heritage of both traditions in its art, architecture, and culture.

*My grace is sufficient for you, for my power
is made perfect in weakness.*

—SECOND CORINTHIANS 12:9

In the late 1970's protestant Christians began to recover the
practice of imposing ashes at the liturgies on Ash Wednesday.
I was in seminary at the time, and one of my classmates
and his spouse brought their 18-month-old daughter to the
noon liturgy. They had taken a seat in the back in case she
became restless during the service. Their choice of seat also
meant that their family was the last to come forward in the
long line to receive ashes. Draped over her father's shoulder,

I can only imagine what it must have looked like to her to see a room full of worshipers with black crosses imposed on our foreheads. We must have looked like a living cemetery.

As the presider gently moved that thin, blond baby hair to sign her with the cross, she screamed. There is no other way to say it. She screamed, breaking the silence and the solemnity of this moment. Her response was more potent than any sermon that could have been preached that day. She spoke for all of us. "No! No! No!" Was all she said. But we all knew what she meant. She did not want to look like the rest of us. She did not want to be marked with the sign of death. She did not want to be reminded of her mortality. None of us did.

Imagine what it must have been like for those few brave men and women to linger around the foot of the cross and release the body of Jesus from the cross. No mortal wants to be reminded of his or her death. Certainly no mortals want to be holding the lifeless body of the one whom they believe to be the author and giver of life. Yet there they were, holding his lifeless, formless, limp, pale, dead body. "No! No! No!" their hearts must have screamed. Perhaps their voices did as well.

And yet it was from the weakness of this ashen, cold, dead body that the grace of God would stir and bring new life to all the world.

The opportunity to see beyond the weakness of death and into the hope of new life is a gift that the cross of Jesus offers to the faithful.

"Remember that you are dust, and to dust you shall return." They seem like words of condemnation, and yet they are the words that contain in them the kernel of the

Gospel's truth. For from the ashes of death the Crucified Christ will raise up all the world to a new creation. This is the promise and the hope of Good Friday. It is the power that is made perfect in the weakness of Jesus' surrender to death.

∾

Gracious God, in the wonder and mystery of your death on the cross you make all things new. In our sin we refuse to accept our own mortality and we live under the illusion that we are able to somehow save ourselves. Forgive us for our selfish pride. Help us to see that it is only by your death that we have any hope at all to overcome our human weakness and be raised up with you to new life. And help us, we pray, to know that it is your grace alone that is sufficient to answer every need.

We ask this through Christ our Lord. Amen

Station Ten

Jesus is laid in the tomb

After these things, Joseph of Arimathea, who was a disciple of Jesus, though a secret one because of his fear of the Jews, asked Pilate to let him take away the body of Jesus. Pilate gave him permission; so he came and removed his body. Nicodemus, who had at first come to Jesus by night, also came, bringing a mixture of myrrh and aloes, weighing about a hundred pounds. They took the body of Jesus and wrapped it with the spices in linen cloths, according to the burial custom of the Jews. Now there was a garden in the place where he was crucified, and in the garden there was a new tomb in which no one had ever been laid. And so, because it was the Jewish day of Preparation, and the tomb was nearby, they laid Jesus there.

—John 19:38–42

ONCE AGAIN we find ourselves the benefactors of the work of British sculptor Eric Gill. This, the final station, is also located in the Roman Catholic Westminster Cathedral in London, England.

Of note in this station's interpretation by the artist is the gold-leafed halos borne by each one of the participants in Christ's burial.

Usually, such adornments are reserved in classic artwork for Jesus, and occasionally Joseph and Mary as well. One might interpret this to be a fulfillment of Christ's own words, "And I, when I am lifted up from the earth will draw all people to myself." (John 12:32) The crucifixion accomplished, the work of God is indeed finished as Jesus has attested from the cross. The salvation of the world and the renewal of creation have begun.

~

This is my commandment, that you love one another
as I have loved you.

—JOHN 15:12

There are no statistics to prove it, but more words are spoken among airline passengers during the last five minutes of a flight than there were the previous three hours combined. As the landing gear goes down and the tray tables go up, the conversations begin. "So are you home now?" "Are you vacationing here or traveling for business?" ". . . was a pretty good flight, don't you think?"

The previous hours seemed simply too much of a risk or commitment for most people. But now when time is short and the prospect of entanglements lowered, our need to connect overrides our fear. "I'm Bud Smith. I've lived here in the Bay Area for twenty years. I hope you enjoy your stay."

It isn't until Jesus has died that Joseph of Arimathea steps out of the shadows of Scripture's pages. If he had been around for the previous weeks and months of Jesus' ministry, we never hear about him. Like weary travelers whose defenses are worn down, his need to connect with Christ now overrides his fear. The risks seem lower now. What could happen by simply offering a tomb and an honorable burial? He is able to reach out to Christ in death in a way that he could not while Christ was still alive.

Unlike Joseph, and certainly unlike us, Christ risks it all for the world. He doesn't wait for a time of safety, but from the very beginning of his ministry reaches to those in need and risks whatever entanglements may result: social, political, religious.

The opportunity to extend ourselves to others in love is a gift that the cross of Jesus offers to the faithful.

We can never repay Jesus for what he has done for us in his life, death, and resurrection. But life in Christ does offer us the opportunity to bury our fear deep in the borrowed grave of his love. Jesus alone can take our fear and reticence and raise up in their place the possibility of new relationships, opportunities, and challenges. To care for one another is to live the resurrected life.

As followers of Jesus and people of faith there is no reason to wait until the plane is landing, that perceived time of safety and lowered risk. The time to care for one another in the name of the Crucified Jesus is now, for Christ's sake.

∼

Gracious God, we often fail to reach out to one another in love, fearing the costs and complications that relationships with others might bring. We are grateful that you do not count the cost of loving us, but offer yourself to us, even to the point of giving your life. Help us to bury our fears in the confidence that you will raise us up in courage and commitment as we share what you have first given us—life itself—with a world in need.

We ask this through Christ our Lord. Amen.